Great and Little Shelford

in old picture postcards

by
Margaret K. Ward

European Library – Zaltbommel/Netherlands

Acknowledgements:
The author thanks all friends and relatives who live, or have lived, in Great or Little Shelford, and have helped in the production of this book by lending photographs and giving information for the text. Sincere thanks also to Mike Petty and his staff of the Cambridgeshire Collection, who have made available such a wealth of material, and also to Michael Rouse for his encouragement and support.

Bibliography:
V.C.H., Cambs.
A Record of the Shelfords, F.L. Wale.
Rose Macaulay, Constance Babington Smith.
Father, S. Campion.
James Thomason, Richard Temple.
Domesday to Dormitory. Ed. C.C. Taylor.

GB ISBN 90 288 5504 1 / CIP

INTRODUCTION

A very pleasant spot, where there are two bridges – close to that is our mansion, with walks extending down to the river – a more beautiful place I never saw; it is the garden of Cambridgeshire! Thus wrote Thomas Thomason c1800 of his home in Little Shelford.

The two parishes of Great and Little Shelford are situated on either side of the River Cam, or Granta. It was from the shallow ford found at this crossing point of the river between the two settlements that the name of Shelford was derived. There are two branches of the river at this point and it was not until the late 14th century that wooden bridges were built and a causeway was raised to cross the marshy ground between them. The villages developed over the centuries, each with its own distinct identity, and even today there are few similarities between them.

Great Shelford, to the east of the original river crossing, has twice as much land within its parish boundaries as its western neighbour and this land has been crossed by several important road routes from early times, but it was the arrival of the railway in the mid-19th century that really changed the face of Great Shelford. New to the village were the employees of the Railway Company – stationmaster, porters, signalmen, gatekeepers, linesmen, etc. – many of these coming from distant parts of the country where they had already gained experience of the workings of the railways. With the journey to Cambridge now only taking a few minutes, there was an influx of professional people who chose to make their homes in the country houses, with large gardens, which were being built both within the village or in the surrounding open countryside. So Great Shelford ceased being the insular unit that it had become over the centuries, when population movement was generally between villages in the immediate vicinity. But inhabitants adapted to the changes and the old-established businesses expanded and flourished, and new firms developed to cater for the needs of the growing population. As housing development spread with the passing years along Cambridge Road, Great Shelford lost its feeling of isolation and was fast becoming a suburb of Cambridge. Whereas the majority of villagers had, in the past, found their employment within the confines of the parish, now commuting was becoming a word that many people understood. The population figures show that Great Shelford almost doubled in size in the forty years from 1891 when a figure of 1,020 is given, and 1931 when the figure stood at 1,864. During this same period Little Shelford shows a slight drop in population with 494 in 1891 and 440 in 1931. Life beyond the Water Bridges was not expanding to the same extent. Although able to take advantage of the presence of Shelford Station, Little Shelford life was not influenced by it and village life continued at a more leisurely, less competitive pace.

In this book I have hoped to depict life in Great and Little Shelford from the end of the 1800s up to 1930. Days when pleasures were simple and most entertainment was found within the village. At the annual Village Feast, which in Little Shelford was held around the Prince Regent, there was dancing in the evening and during the day villagers jostled amongst the fairground rides, booths and stalls that lined Church Street. Great Shelford Flower Show and Gala was a day to anticipate as July approached. Held on the recreation ground it was a grand affair with a band playing, athletic sports, a baby show, country dancing, sideshows, as well as numerous classes for amateur and professional gardeners. May Day was another highlight of the year, as were the traditional country church festivals such as Rogationtide, Plough

Monday and, of course, Harvest. Many clubs and societies flourished, bearing names such as Comrades of the Great War and the Women's Friendly League. There was much fund-raising for worthwhile causes, and garden parties and fêtes were organised for the summer months with slide shows and lectures to fill the dark winter evenings.

This was the world of my grandfathers, when occupations such as higgler, fly proprietor, milliner, stocking knitter, hemp maker and strawplait maker were worthy of an entry in the Shelford pages of Kelly's Trade Directory. Fanny Wale records: *In 1911 two aeroplanes passed over the Shelfords.* Quite a spectacle! And five years earlier she mentions the sighting of a motorcar in the village. By 1930 both planes and cars were becoming commonplace and radio was in everyone's home.

When the author Rose Macaulay wrote to a friend after her family had moved to Great Shelford from Wales, she was scathing about the flatness of the landscape. *There are at least three mountains in our neighbourhood quite six feet high (the Gog Magog Hills), so we ought to be contented. The natives regard them as young Alps. We mistook them for mole-hills at first: we have to be very guarded in our language on the subject when we converse with the inhabitants.*

Her friend Rupert Brooke also mentioned the village in his poem 'The Old Vicarage, Grantchester'. He wrote: *And folks in Shelford and those parts / Have twisted lips and twisted hearts.* Not very complimentary! But this we do know, that both of these writers spent many happy times together in the locality before the outbreak of the First World War. Rupert Brooke sadly was a victim of the conflict, but Rose in her old age looked back to her years at Great Shelford and described them as 'that Golden Age'. In more modern times Philippa

Pearce, whose father Ernest owned King's Mill, found such delight in her childhood surroundings that she was inspired to write 'Tom's Midnight Garden' and 'Minnow on the Tay', both of which draw on memories of happy days on and around the River Granta.

I spent my childhood at Four Mile House, as did S. Campion, author of 'Father − a picture of G.G. Coulton'. Her thoughts of the village over a period of eleven years are very evocative, and a description of the last winter of the First World War coincides with my own memories of the last winter of the Second World War. *My last memory of Shelford is of winter, deep winter and hard frost. All the village has come to skate, slide, slither and tumble on our pond; we feel very much in the public eye. Warmly muffled figures, only dark blurs in the distance but recognisable at a few yards, swoop back and forth across the wonderful soapy glimmer of the ice: someone has brought a lantern, and threads its light back and forth by the slide the children have made near the railway line.* Yes, I remember it, as will other Shelford people who dared to venture on the Ballast Hole behind Four Mile House!

In my selection of pictures I have aimed to take the reader on a journey through the two villages, showing scenes which will bring back memories to older residents, and for those who did not know Great and Little Shelford in the years before 1930, an insight into the recent history and a bygone age.

Maris Farm, Great Shelford,
September 1992.   Margaret Ward

1. There was very little development along the Cambridge Road until the 1920's and so the two-mile journey from Trumpington to Great Shelford would have been through open farmland, with only the occasional house. The first of the eight public houses in the village of Great Shelford – The Greyhound – would no doubt have been a welcome sight to many thirsty travellers in the days at the beginning of the century. The road bends to the left and rises over the Northern bridge, which was built to carry the traffic over the Cambridge to King's Cross railway line in 1851. The view beyond stretches across meadows to the distant cottages in Granham's Road, whilst the track to the right indicates the line of the original road, and it was here that the turnpike milestone stood indicating four miles to Cambridge.

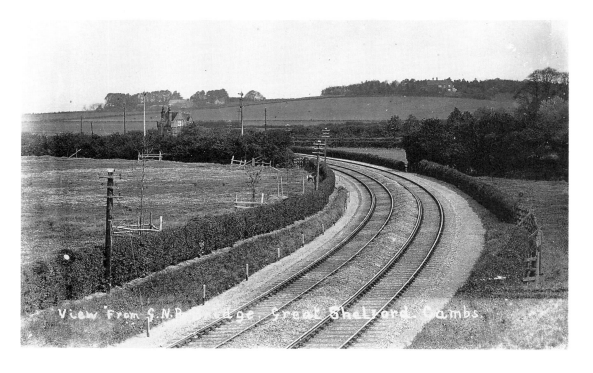

View from G.N.R. Bridge, Great Shelford, Cambs.

2. This view from the Great Northern bridge looks across open fields to the distant hills. The daisy-strewn meadow was to be developed as The Crescent, and the field on the right was to become Granham's Close at a later date. In the middle distance stands Junction House, built at the point where the Liverpool Street and King's Cross railway lines merge. It was the home of the railway signalman and it was approached through a white-painted hand gate near the crossing in Granham's Road. Nine Wells House stands amongst woodland on the summit of White Hill. It was built for Sir Michael Foster at the end of the last century and affords distant views to the south as far as Royston Heath. White Hill Farm, with its large chalk, or clunch, barn, is situated on the lower slopes of the hill.

3. The railway gates in Granham's Road were manned by the crossing keeper, who lived in the bungalow on the left. This small, but attractive, brick and slate building was typical of all the gate keepers' houses along this stretch of track. In previous centuries this road was known as Hollow Willow Back Road and it is along here that the village clay pit and also the chalk, or clunch, pit were to be found. This roadway would have been in frequent use as the local people collected these materials, to build or repair their houses or farm buildings. A favourite summer walk was to Nine Wells, the source of Hobson's Brook in Cambridge, which is to be found along a footpath to the north of Granham's Road. These springs arise at the base of the chalk hill amongst a thicket of hawthorn and brambles.

Gt. Shelford Feast 1920
⑤

4. The Village Feast was the highlight of the month of July and attracted folk of all ages from far and near. In 1920 Ted Mott took a series of photographs of this event when it was held as usual in the field at the rear of the De Freville public house. Thurstons' Fair travelled throughout East Anglia and when they came to Shelford they brought the latest in rides, amusements and sideshows. The Gallopers, seen here, the swingboats, hoopla, coconut shie, rifle range, Try your strength. Roll up, roll up, plenty for everyone! Shivery and Amy Wright travelled for about forty years with Thurstons, living in their wooden waggon which in the early days was drawn by a piebald horse and later on by a giant traction engine. The Wrights chose to retire to Great Shelford and their caravan still stands only a hundred yards from the site of the Village Feast.

8873 High St. Great Shelford.

5. This photograph depicts a leisurely way of life on High Green in the early years of the century. At the turn of the century Alfred Marfleet, master saddler and harness maker, worked and sold his wares from his shop next to the Post Office. In 1921 his son was still practising this craft, although no doubt he could see that the motor car was taking over from the horse and already there were two motor car garages in the village. The flint wall on the right fronts the garden of Malyons, the butchers, and beyond this is the house of Edward Webb, master blacksmith. The signpost marks the end of High Green, with High Street bearing off to the right and thus onto Little Shelford, whilst Tunwell's Lane continues on towards Stapleford with the tall trees of The Chestnuts bordering its left-hand side.

6. 'Established 1765' was proudly displayed on the large sign board at the end of Malyons' driveway on High Green. 'All home-killed English meat.' Young Samuel Malyon, aged 21, sits atop this smart turnout in the cobbled yard behind the shop. The year is 1898. Samuel was to meet an untimely death in 1915, in one of the first motor car fatalities, leaving his wife to continue the business until her sons were of an age to take over. Before refrigeration Mr. Malyon would select and buy various animals either from local farmers or at the cattle market, which he would then bring back to Shelford to graze in the field behind the shop until such time as they were needed to be slaughtered and sold. George and Frank Malyon retired in 1978 and the house is now a private home, appropriately called 'Malyons'.

7. 'Their names liveth for evermore.' The memorial cross was unveiled by the Lord Lieutenant (Mr. C. Adeane) on 2nd January 1921 in front of a large congregation including comrades of the Great War and other ex-servicemen, the Girl Guides and members of the V.A.D. In his address Mr. Adeane appealed 'for the same spirit to be shown at the present time which obtained during the war'. Then the names of the forty-three men and women who had given their lives for their country were read by Mr. W. de Devereux. Behind the memorial can be seen The Elms, a large house built around 1850. At this time it was occupied by William Sindall, who gave the ground on which the memorial was placed. The house is now demolished, but sections of the garden wall can still be seen in High Street and Tunwell's Lane.

8806   High Street Gt. Shelford

8. Several of the publicans in the village followed a second occupation. Such a man was Henry J. How, landlord of The Plough, who also had a bakehouse to the rear of the building. In the 1891 census returns he was living there with his 46-year-old wife, Harriet, and their ten children with ages ranging from 21 to 4 years. The public house flourished, as did the baker's business, and today we can still see evidence of the entrepreneurial success of Henry and his family, for in 1906 he was able to build a modern brick house on ground adjoining The Plough. This building stands largely unaltered in external appearance, 'H.J.H. 1906', engraved on the gable end, as a memorial to this energetic man. It has for many years been the village branch of Lloyds Bank.

8809   The Cross   Shelford

9. In the fifty years up to 1901 around sixty houses were built in the parish. The majority of these were large residences, built to accommodate members of the professional classes, who were now able to travel to Cambridge in a few minutes from Shelford Station — a journey that would have taken an hour by horse-drawn transport. Chestnut House was just such a house. In 1900 Mr. George Foster was living there, but during the First World War it was used as a Red Cross Hospital for military personnel. It became known as Browning House later on and for many years was a private girls' school with Miss Tidey as headmistress. The grounds then stretched from Tunwell's Lane to the railway line and station and it was not unusual to see a uniformed crocodile of schoolgirls coming through the kissing-gate in Station Road to catch the train into town.

8807 High Street Gt. Shelford.

10. A pair of cottages stood on the pavement edge next to The Plough. These were built of clay bat with flint foundations — building materials which would have been available locally. Clay bats were used for many of the smaller houses and farm buildings and were made by mixing clay with straw and placing this mixture in a wooden mould, where it was left to dry naturally. They gave thick walls with good insulation, but the exterior rendering needed constant maintenance to avoid the effects of frost and rain. Sam Rolph, boot repairer, stands with a friend outside his shop and in the distance can be seen the Square and Compasses, an old timber-framed house which was encased in brick at a later date.

High St. Gt. Shelford

11. A small group of children standing in the centre of the road, heedless of the oncoming cyclists, are trans-
fixed by Mr. Mott and his camera. The nursemaid and her charge, however, take up a safer position in front
of The Grove. This large mid-18th century house was inhabited by Mrs. Robertson for over twenty years.
Beyond the big house a group of five terraced cottages border Pound Yard. In the 1891 census four of these
two-bedroomed homes were each occupied by two or three people, while the fifth housed a family of
eleven, with the children's ages ranging from 3 months to 21 years. The newly-built brick houses which line
the left-hand side of the street stretching as far as Mr. Rolph's shop, were placed on previously open land,
thus completing the link between the oldest part of the village, which originated around the church, and
the other ancient development on High Green.

12. Turning to look southwards down the High Street now we see three thatched cottages that remain to this day. The first with its horizontal sliding sash windows and timber shutter has a small shop belonging to A.F. Morley on the land adjoining. The next thatched cottage, standing endways to the road, was originally a farmhouse, but was later divided into two. Mrs. Acker had a small sweet shop opening onto the footpath and Reuben and Susan Goat with their family lived at the other end of the house. Reuben had learnt his trade of a carpenter from his grandfather and he passed his skills onto his sons, Reuben and Fred. As was usual in a village, the carpenter was also the undertaker and an old invoice written by Reuben (jr.) tells us that the cost of a funeral in 1921 was £7.17.6d.

13. This old photograph, dated at 1900 and showing only the shop front of Hope & Co., is at first difficult to place in the village scene. However, by comparing it with the picture following, it can be seen that this is the same building — the cornices, the shop window design and the paving on the road edge is the same in both pictures but there is possibly a lapse of around twenty years between them. What a variety of goods can be seen in Mr. Hope's windows, but it does seem that the photographer arrived before he could complete his display on the outside staging. Four hoops are hanging up waiting for a youthful buyer, and there is a selection of stone jars — whether full or empty we cannot tell. To the right are bundles of plants, possibly for hedging, but had he intended to place more of his wares on the wooden crates? We shall never know!

High St. Gt. Shelford

14. A new fascia board and a coat of paint transforms Hope's shop into The Central Stores, which was run by C.G. Butler at this time (c1920). General provisions were sold, but there is very little sign of any trade with the almost deserted High Street. Perhaps it is the dinner hour? The imposing columns of Porch House can be seen behind the iron railings on the right. Beyond can be seen the end gable of a group of buildings that stretched back from the road alongside a yard. This was used by a corn merchant at one time. In Kelly's Directory of 1922 there are four corn merchants listed in Great Shelford, evidence that the soil on local farms is well-suited to cereal growing.

High St. Great Shelford.

15. The Baptist Chapel on the east side of the High Street was built in 1856 on land given by Richard W. Maris. Built in yellow and red brick and designed to seat 470 people, the chapel replaced a smaller meeting house which had stood in Church Street. The Manse was built in 1896 and until this was completed, the Minister lived at Ferndale, the house opposite the chapel. In 1912 a large schoolroom was built at the rear and since then there have been several other alterations and additions. Adjoining the chapel grounds are the gardens of Porch House which can just be seen through the trees. On the opposite side of the road the baker's horse waits patiently as deliveries are made from the cart.

16. 'Cocks & Childs Family Butchers' is written above the shop window, whilst on display to tempt the passing housewife hangs a variety of joints and strings of sausages. Mr. Cocks stands in blue and white striped apron, knife and steel in hand ready to return to the side of beef which can be seen on the chopping block inside. His assistant, still wearing his cap, has possibly just returned on his tradesman's cycle from delivering orders. This business was just one of four family butchers that could be found in the village at this time and the shop was built on land adjoining the Manse — the end wall of the house can be seen behind the wooden fence.

17. The striped sunblind is down over the window at Miller Barker's butcher's shop: a long-established business which has carried on through the generations and is still trading from the same premises today. Jack and Peter White with their cart pulled by two donkeys were a common sight around the village. They came from Stapleford and dealt in oil and other sundries. The young boy in his Norfolk jacket has just had his gallon can filled with paraffin, an essential in many households for cooking – particularly during the summer months, when a small economy could be made by not lighting the kitchen range. The pantiled cottages stood around an area known at one time as Chapel Yard. These and the adjoining brick-built houses with their attractive porches have now gone.

High St. Great Shelford.

18. The meeting of three roads — High Street, Church Street and Woollard's Lane. The signpost indicates only Shelford Station as it points eastwards — no mention is made of the villages in that direction such as Cherry Hinton, Stapleford or Sawston. The children crossing the road could be making for Jesse Garner's sweet shop when a penn'orth of sweets could be chosen from the tempting array of jars. Later this low thatched cottage was to become the Bluebird Café with Mrs. Bridgeman in charge. Further down the street Oak Cottage borders the road, its casement windows wide open and as yet the oak beams on its jettied upper storey not yet exposed. When restoration work was carried out on this 16th century timber-framed house, some very fine folded leaf carving was uncovered on the exterior.

19. Although seen here as the Shelford Garage this large building at the junction of Woollard's Lane and Church Street was previously known as the British School. It was erected in 1870 with accommodation for 150 children (although it seems unlikely that it ever reached that figure); by 1900 the attendance was 54. The British School was closed in 1906 and the remaining pupils transferred to the church school. For some years it was used as a meeting room. Around 1920 it was sold to Frederick Pumfrey, who had been running a small garage business nearby and was eager to acquire larger premises to cater for the growing demands of the increasing number of car owners. An interesting collection of cars can be seen on the forecourt behind the iron railings. Mr. Pumfrey himself owned a Rolls Royce.

station Rd. Gr. Shelford.

20. With the coming of the railway and Shelford Station, Woollard's Lane had been renamed Station Road and it continued with this name until the 1920's, when it reverted to its original title. Here we see that the milk roundsman, Billy Bye, had progressed from a horse-drawn milk float to a motorised van. James Edwin Rodwell farmed at Rectory Farm for many years. His land stretched from Church Street along the River Granta towards Hauxton and it was on these lush meadows that his herd of cows grazed. George C. Williams, often known as Nanny Williams, had run the general stores and draper's shop since the beginning of the century. The next shop along the street was for many years a hardware store under the ownership of Miss Litton.

7876 Station Rd. Great Shelford

21. This photograph can be accurately dated to 1916 by reading the newsagent's bill-boards. 'Brilliant victories on Somme' says the Chronicle board. What feelings would this news arouse in the hearts of wives and mothers with their loved ones far away in France? 'Zeppelin shot down' and in the Daily Mail 'Zeppelin special pictures'. No doubt George Bros, the newsagents, had a great demand for the national papers at this anxious time as they were the main means of communication with events in the Great War. The sign board high on the wall above the shop states 'George Bros Florists and Nurserymen', a trade for which they were well-known for many years. Their glasshouses and gardens were behind the shop.

22. The memory of Robinson's herd of Jersey cows wandering their twice daily journey between the dairy in Woollard's Lane and the water-meadows of The Grange and King's Mill would epitomise for many people all that was fresh, clean and wholesome in village life in those quieter, less hurried years between the wars. However, those with longer memories will know that before embarking into the dairy business Mr. Eliab Robinson and his son Alfred had been well-respected builders and carpenters in the village. Upto 1930 there were four boot-makers and repairers in the village. Frederick Dyne started such a business in the 1920's, when he rented a small wooden shop in Mr. Robinson's front garden. Charles Butler of Little Shelford sells his crusty homebaked bread from the shop next door.

23. Miss Dorothy Bockham, listed in Kelly's Directory as a 'Patent Medicine Vendor', was a source of much help and comfort to the ailing members of the community. Her small wooden shop — The Welfare Drug Store — stood opposite the Recreation Ground and through the trees the old corrugated iron village hall can be seen. In the distance is the signboard of Josiah Austin, the local builder, who was living at Flowerdale in the 1920's when this picture was taken. Previously he had lived with his family in premises on High Green and he was responsible for the building of a number of houses in Great Shelford in the early part of the century. It is recorded that in 1791 the earliest clay bat domestic building in England was erected here by Joseph Austin. An ancestor of Josiah's perhaps?

7877 Southernwood Gt. Shelford.

24. In 1906 George Macaulay came with his family to live at Southernwood. With him came his daughter Rose, then aged 25, who had already completed her first novel. In later years Rose recalled these years before the war as 'that Golden Age', when much of her time was spent in the company of the poet Rupert Brooke, a family friend. They spent time together and Rose continued to write both novels and poetry. With the outbreak of war Rose volunteered as a nurse at Mount Blow (Stapleford), a military convalescent home. She did not enjoy the work and was far happier when she became a landgirl working for Peter Grain at Station Farm in Hinton Way. The experience inspired her to write a collection of poems called 'On the Land 1916', which recall the hard work and companionship of those days.

25. Mrs. Grace Macaulay's Bible Class in the garden at Southernwood, 1915. From the left, standing: Daisy Austin, Doris Pettit, unknown, Madge Larkin, Nellie Litchfield and Elsie Dickerson. Seated on chairs: Emily Brunning, unknown, Alice Pryor, Sybil Hiner, Winnie Bowtell and Mary Andrews. Seated on grass: Maud Freeman, Doris Ellis, unknown, Kathleen Marfleet and Millie Ryder. This class was held once a week in a hut in the garden. When the Bible lesson came to an end Mrs. Macaulay would call Rose to take the girls for recreational activities. They canoed and went for rides in the donkey cart and then before leaving for home the girls were given permission to pick their mothers a posy of flowers from the garden at Southernwood.

26. For over twenty-five years Charles Whitmore carried on his two trades of publican and wheelwright from these premises, The Road and Rail public house, which stood on the junction of Woollard's Lane and London Road. Coming down the slope from the railway bridge we see two types of horse-drawn vehicles. The milk float, possibly belonging to Charles Clay of Manor Farm, Little Shelford, and a smart carriage with liveried coachman which may have belonged to Dr. Magoris, who lived in The Woodlands. Again we see the White brothers from Stapleford with their donkey cart. The land on the opposite corner was sold as a building plot in 1902 and it was bought by George Freestone, who had built a splendid house, shop and bakery to replace the older premises that he was using in Woollard's Lane.

27. When the Cambridge to Liverpool Street railway line came through the village in 1845, a triangle of farmland belonging to Richard Headley became isolated from the remainder of his land. This ground is bordered by the railway, Station Road and London Road. Mr. Headley took full advantage of the presence of this new form of transport by building a large brewery, maltings and coalstore around a yard which had access to railway sidings. Around the turn of the century Mr. Martin Wright and Clarence George were joint proprietors of the business now known as the Shelford Corn and Coal Company. The firm came into the sole ownership of the George family at a later date and here we see one of their early Morris lorries which were used for house-to-house coal deliveries.

28. Here we see the Railway Tavern, again built by Mr. Headley, who could see that with the arrival of the railway station and sidings and the new developments around this area, there would be a lot of thirsts to be quenched! Certainly sometime around the 1920's the Road and Rail closed and so the nearest public house was the Black Swan in Church Street. This picture, taken c1930, shows a building that is hardly recognisable today. The attractive bay windows have gone and the gardens have been replaced by the inevitable car park. The end of a range of buildings around the Corn and Coal Co. yard can just be glimpsed and the newly erected semi-detached houses in Station Road are evident.

29. This view of the station level-crossing was taken c1904. A horse and cart laden with sacks wait patiently whilst Great Eastern Railway's locomotive No. 761 stands in the station. This engine was often used to pull Royal trains until it was scrapped in 1908. On 6th June 1893 it drew the train taking the Duke and Duchess of York, later King George V and Queen Mary, from Liverpool Street to King's Lynn for their honeymoon at Sandringham. The lowered signal indicates that this train is heading for London, not the Haverhill line which branches off a few hundred yards down the track. Beyond the station buildings can be seen open ground and the rear of the newly built houses in Tunwell's Lane.

Hinton Way, Great Shelford.

30. Before returning to the hub of the village, we take a long, last look along Hinton Way as it stretches off into the distance, over Clarke's Hill which rises to 45 metres, and so onto Shelford Bottom. In the early years of the century this was a remote area of the parish, which stretched to Wandlebury, Worts Causeway and Red Cross. Maybe the farmers and smallholders felt that they had a greater affinity with Cambridge than with Great Shelford. Nevertheless, the children had to walk to and from the village school each day, the one concession being that they could take a packed lunch. In 1900 the golf course was laid out on around 200 acres of the Gog Magog Hills. Near this point the village lime kiln was to be found in the hillside.

31. Mr. Linsey boasts twenty years experience in the cycle trade, the coach house and stables stand waiting in the yard of the Black Swan, but the young men have their minds on other forms of transport. They pose for the photographer around a sporty open two-seater car. One takes the wheel whilst another swings the starting handle. Mr. Linsey looks apprehensively around the door of his workshop, but he needn't worry, it will be many years before the ordinary working man will be able to afford a car and his cycle trade looks set to continue for another twenty years. And who is the owner of this splendid vehicle? Could it be the gentleman in the light coloured coat and homburg hat standing in the background, who is tolerating the high spirits of the local lads?

8256 High St. Great Shelford

32. This view down Church Street shows the Black Swan (or Mucky Duck as it was frequently called by the locals!). This inn is recorded as far back as 1791, when an advertisement was placed in the Cambridgeshire Chronicle, saying that a farmhouse was to be auctioned at 'the sign of the Black Swan'. Where the street bears around to the right stands The Grange behind its flint and brick wall. Built on the site of an earlier Manor House parts of this house date back to the 16th century, but it was extended in 1890 when the Grain family sold it to Mr. Carter Jonas. There is a range of interesting outbuildings, including a granary and a brewhouse. The gardens are attractively landscaped and stretch back to the banks of the River Granta.

Church St. Great Shelford.

33. This picture was taken around 1916. Later Elm Cottage was demolished, to make way for the new vicarage that was to be built on this site in 1929. Whilst waiting for the new house to be completed the vicar, Reverend Frederic Jeeves, lived next door in the Red House, as the Victorian vicarage adjoining the church had already been sold into private ownership. Reverend Jeeves had come to the village as a curate in 1913 to assist Reverend Nettleship and at this time he resided at Hope Cottage in Church Street. He served as vicar for twenty-six years. On the opposite side of the road stands The Peacock with its painted sign depicting this colourful bird. From the late 1800's E.K. & H. Fordham ran the Brewery Stores from this site. In 1916 George Flint was the manager of this business, which had connections with Ashwell Brewery.

34. A small thatched cottage stands on the pavement edge partly obscuring the entrance into the Old Vicarage, and standing on a slight rise in the ground is the village church. Dating back to the 14th century and dedicated to St. Mary the Virgin it has numerous interesting features, many of which have been added over the centuries. The three timber-framed and plastered cottages opposite the church entrance were built around 1600 and were originally one large farmhouse. Kerbing along the footpath edge, white lines in the centre of the road, a school warning sign − all of these are indications that the age of the motorised vehicle was taking over from slower moving horse-drawn traffic.

35. The National School, as it was once known, was erected around 1840 to provide free education for boys and girls from Great and Little Shelford. The average attendance in 1900 was 193 pupils. From 1906 it became known as Great and Little Shelford Church of England School and until Sawston Village College was opened in 1930 the village children spent their entire school career here. This group photograph was taken in 1911 when Mr. Charles Smith was headmaster. He had the reputation of being kind but very strict and during his time at Shelford he was also organist and choirmaster. Among the names remembered by Nellie Litchfield (third row back, third from left) are: Mary Andrews, Dolly Austin, Madge Larkin, Ethel Hiner, Doris Pettit, Bert Taylor, Fred Linsey and Wilfred Marfleet.

Great Shelford

36. This postcard printed by Stanley, Talbot & Co. of Linton shows a winter scene in Church Street c1900. The thatched house on the right was used as a club for the young men of the village in the early part of the century. Previously it had been the George and Dragon inn, but the latest record of this was in 1859. The group of three thatched cottages on the corner of King's Mill Lane have long been demolished. Mr. and Mrs. Gifford lived in the end cottage with their daughter Nell, who was a talented amateur photographer. She took many photographs around the village which she developed and printed in primitive conditions in her parents' cottage. Her aim seemed to have been to record the people, not just a scene, and she was prepared to take a photograph of loved-ones in their coffin if so requested.

37. This picture taken by Nell Gifford just a few yards from her home shows Francis Litchfield and his son Frank returning to Little Shelford with their timber waggon. Frank, aged 15, holds the lead horse and pauses whilst Nell takes her photograph. They are just returning from Shelford Station, where they have been to collect a load of wood − possibly for Edward Walker, carpenter and builder, as the man with the bike is one of his workmen. Much of the wood used by local carpenters came from the yard of English at Wisbech as it could easily be transported by rail to the station sidings in the village. The thatched building on the left is the end of a row of five small cottages which have since been demolished.

Mill Lane, Great Shelford.

38. A distant view across the meadows in King's Mill Lane to the church and Rutland House with a varied group of cottages to the left. The lane is suprisingly deserted, usually it would be busy with carts rumbling to and from Pearce's Mill. The first mention of a mill on this site was in 1086 when it was the property of the Abbot of Ely and it is also recorded that there was a second water-mill in Great Shelford, although its position is unknown. Local people believed that it had been further along the Granta at Hopping (or Hopham) where traces of brickwork could be seen bordering the river. Another mill was to be found in the village. This was Chaston's Flour Mill and it developed with the coming of the railway. Built adjoining the station it could take full advantage of this form of transport.

Near Kings Mill, Great Shelford.

39. A tranquil scene across the millpond to the cottages built in the early 19th century to house some of the men who were employed at King's Mill. This mill had been built on the site of an ancient water-mill along the River Granta and in 1875 it was taken over from Josiah Living by Alexander Pearce, miller and farmer, who had been born at Shepreth 29 years earlier. In the 1890's Alexander updated the mill by adding roller machinery, turbines and installing an engine house, so that he was no longer entirely dependant upon water power. In 1922 the Pearce family were able to buy the mill from Gonville and Caius, who had owned it since 1614. Ernest Pearce, Alexander's son, continued to run the business and at the same time served for forty years as Chairman of the Parish Council and twenty years as a J.P.

40. The lane gently slopes down towards the river, passing on the right a group of three cottages which were originally built as one house. A decorative plaque can be seen on the front wall of the house engraved with 'R.K. 1738'. However, this was probably the date of alterations rather than the date of construction, as plasterwork on one of the bedroom ceilings gave the date of 1676 in the centre of a diamond shaped crest. Although these were the last houses in the village at the time of the photograph, a Turnpike Cottage and gate stood on the distant corner until 1871, when the County Council took over the care of the roads. Road surfaces were still very loose and dusty well into this century and heaps of chippings were placed at frequent intervals on the roadside for on-the-spot repairs!

Shelford Bridges.

41. The Water Bridges provide a natural boundary between the two villages, one river being attributed to Great Shelford and the other to Little Shelford. Fanny Wale recalls that a line was marked on the wall between the rivers and here village boys met to fight on their own village boundary. In this picture we look towards Great Shelford and the nearest bridge crosses the original path of the River Granta or Cam, whilst the other channel is said to have been excavated by the miller in order to increase the flow of water through his mill − hence its straight course through the water meadows. This land is very low-lying and prone to flooding after heavy rain so that the two rivers merge.

8269 Bridge Rd. Shelford.

42. And so we enter Little Shelford. Bridge Lane is little changed from the scene shown in this photograph taken seventy years ago. The 18th century red brick wall on the left borders the grounds of the Manor, the Manor House itself being hidden in the trees. The buttressed wall on the right hides from view the gardens of Shelford Hall. The village spread from a nucleus that had developed in this area, including the Manor and the church. It grew westwards along Church Street and then turned south into High Street, previously known as Thames Street Road in the early 19th century. There was also some growth north-west towards Hauxton, Newton and Harston. This framework of the development of housing remained with little alteration well into this century.

The Manor House, Little Shelford

43. The Georgian Manor House stands in a secluded position in Manor Lane. From the late 13th century it was the main seat of the De Freville family, but after three hundred years they sold it to Tobias Palavicino, who built a grand new house on the site. This house was largely demolished c1750 and the present house, designed by the famous architect Inigo Jones, was built. Some material from the previous house, including Palavicino's coat of arms, was incorporated in the new building. At the beginning of this century John Clay M.A., J.P. of Newnham, was Lord of the Manor, and William Walton was living at the Manor House. It later became the property of the Pares Wilsons. Charles Felix Clay lived at Manor Farm for over thirty years from 1900.

44. The Wale family have had connections with Little Shelford over many generations and they were still listed as the principal landowners well into this century. The family seat, known as Shelford Hall or the Old House, was built in the 17th century but this building was largely demolished around 1850 and a new house was erected in the Gothic style. This is the building shown on this postcard and the date stamp indicates that it was posted just a few months before Old Hall was destroyed by fire. Mrs. Eaden was living there at the time — 24th February 1929 — when a fire, believed to have originated in the pantry, gutted the entire building. The roof caved in and there was little chance to retrieve any of the contents. A series of photographs appeared in the Cambridgeshire Chronicle recording this tragedy.

The Lodge, Shelford Hall, Little Shelford.

45. The Lodge to Shelford Hall stands on the corner of Bridge Road and Whittlesford Road and the main entrance and driveway to the Hall adjoins it. This building was the north wing of the original 17th century Hall and it was retained to be used as an entrance lodge to the new house. There is a model of the original building in the possession of the Cambridge and County Folk Museum, although this is not always on public display. The writer of the postcard queries: 'Can you remember going to Sunday School here?' Earlier in the century Miss Fanny Wale had taken Sunday School classes in The Studio, a cottage off the Whittlesford Road, that Col. R.G. Wale had intended to be used as a reading room and adult evening institute.

WITTLESFORD RD.
LITTLE SHELFORD.

46. This postcard, published by the Shelford Supply Stores, was posted in 1921 to Mr. S. Marks in Saffron Walden by his sister. It shows Milestone Cottage, a small, timber-framed house that still retains its picturesque charm today. The milestone, which is just off the picture to the left, tells the traveller that London is 50 miles distant, while Cambridge is 5 miles in the other direction. The wall of Shelford Hall grounds borders the edge of the highway on the right and in the distance through the trees can be seen the Rectory. Hidden from view behind the cottage is an attractive group of small houses, including The Studio, which overlook Camping Close.

6249 Ivy Cottage. L. Shelford.

47. In the year 1900 Fanny Lucretia Wale lived in Ivy Cottage, a low, rambling old house in Whittlesford Road, part-hidden behind a wooden fence and shrubbery. Miss Wale was the last member of the family bearing the name of Wale to live in Little Shelford, and she left a valuable legacy in the form of a book called 'A record of the Shelfords'. She compiled this book between 1907 and 1927 and it provides an excellent record of life in the Shelfords at the beginning of the century. Miss Wale was a competent artist and her book is filled with attractive sketches as well as important historical information, which no doubt she was able to glean from family documents and literature which were available to her. Her meticulous recording of housing and inhabitants is of great interest to the family historian.

Green Lane, Little Shelford.

48. Green Lane, or Whittlesford Road as it is now known, had little development in the early part of the century. Meadowland stretched across from the beech trees on the right to the back gardens of the houses in High Street. The Wale family gave a large area of ground which was behind the wall on the left to be used by the villagers for recreational purposes. The Wale Recreation Ground has a delightful rural setting − edged by long-established deciduous woodland and with the River Cam on its eastern boundary. To the north is the site of Shelford Hall and its gardens. This field is yet another indication of the generosity of the Wale family to the village − a gift that will be appreciated and enjoyed by generations yet to come.

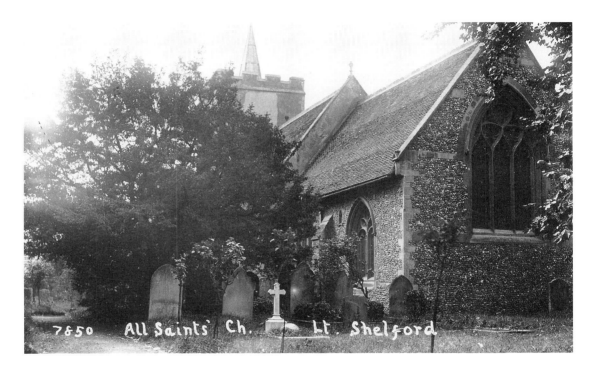

7&50   All Saints' Ch.   Lt. Shelford

49. The Church of All Saints is built of flint with stone dressings. The earliest parts date back to the 12th century and a Norman doorway and window survive in the north wall of the nave. Many alterations and additions have been made over the centuries and a south chapel which was added by Margaret, wife of Thomas de Freville, in the early 15th century, is particularly interesting. Many of the church fittings are associated with the De Freville family and several interesting monumental brasses survive. There are also numerous monuments and inscriptions to commemorate the lives and service of members of the Wale family. In addition to the church there is a small Congregational Chapel, which was founded in 1823 and rebuilt in 1881.

7849 Little Shelford Rectory

50. In 1858 the old Rectory, a long, low building with a deep roof, was demolished. A large, new brick and stone house, built in a Gothic style, was erected on the same site. This work was ordered by the Rector, James Edmund Law, and it is recorded that in 1883 the Rectory was valued at £400. James Law was Rector from 1852 to 1892 and his successor was E.T.S. Carr, who lived at the Rectory until 1929. In 1962 the Rectory shown in the photograph was sold into private ownership and a modern house for the Rector was built further down Manor Road. Many village activities were held in the gardens of the Rectory − fêtes, garden parties, school treats − when everyone would don their best clothes and pray that the fine weather would hold!

8253 Camping Close Little Shelford.

51. This view across Camping Close depicts a peaceful summer's day in the centre of the village c1920. The cattle rest in the shade of the tree and the tower of All Saints' Church can be seen in the distance. The gardens of St. Andrews, in Church Street back onto the meadow and William Garrett Ecclestone was living there at this time. Camping Close was owned by the Wale family, but generally it was rented to a local farmer. Upto 1845 members of the Wale family were buried in a mausoleum which stood in the corner of Camping Close nearest to the church. However, with the prevalence of bodysnatching in those days, which meant that graves needed to be guarded for two months after a funeral, it was decided to move the coffins into a vault in the church.

52. James Thompson was the landlord of The Chequers in Church Street when this picture was taken c1920. The pony and trap provided a leisurely way to travel in those days. I wonder who the gentlemen were who posed for Mr. Mott in this photograph? At the beginning of the century there were six public houses in the village. One of these was the Three Horse Shoes, which stood on the south-east side of Church Street close to the church. It was recorded in 1787 and from the 1891 census returns we know that Albert Smith from Kidlington, near Oxford was the publican. The business survived until 1908 when the building was demolished and a private house was erected on the site. Another hostelry, The William IV in High Street, closed in 1910 and was converted into private houses.

8578 Lt. Shelford Village Hall.

53. This picture by Ted Mott shows the Village Hall, or Institute, that was in use in the early part of the century. It stood, as does the present hall, adjoining the Chequers. This small building was purchased from Whittlesford (perhaps they were having a new hall built?), and transported to Little Shelford by horse and waggon. A collection was made around the village to finance this venture and when they called on the family of the carrier who had transported the hall sections free of charge, they were given a nominal amount of money only. On noting this, the young son of the household laughed and said: 'Well Mother, we shall own the keyhole!' The present hall was erected in 1925 to the memory of the men who fell in the Great War and it was enlarged in 1932 by C.F. Clay of Manor Farm in remembrance of his son, R.V. Clay.

Church St. Little Shelford.

54. Behind these cottages and houses on the right-hand side of Church Street stood the business premises of Galls, which had been established in the village since the mid-18th century. They manufactured rope and twine and at a later date also made sacks and tarpaulins. From the late 19th century tar was also distilled on the premises. This family-run business provided an alternative employment to working on the land and a search through the 1891 census returns shows that nine villagers were giving their occupation as ropemaker. At Great Shelford William Gall was also manufacturing sacks, tarpaulins, rick cloths, cord, etc., but later he diversified to produce gelatine and size.

7837 Church St. Lt. Shelford.

55. At the turn of the century Ephraim Clamp was the postmaster at Little Shelford and the shop was also advertised as selling drapery and groceries. Later Mrs. Sarah Annie Miles and her son were running the Post Office and it is her son, Gillie, with his motor-bike, that we see outside the shop in this picture. An old soldier from either the Boer War or the First World War laughs at Gillie's antics. He wears his army tunic and medals, his left sleeve pinned up as a poignant reminder of his sacrifice for his country. The gentleman standing on the right seems to be a giant of a man − I wonder who he is? By 1930 Miss Minnie Austin was postmistress. Today the villagers must travel to Great Shelford for this service.

9047 Church St. Little Shelford.

56. A winter's scene along Church Street c1920. The trees are bare with the exception of the pine tree in the front garden of Miss Searl's home, Ingleside. The bay window of the Prince Regent can be seen on the left and over the roof of their coach-house can be seen the top of the tall chimney at Gall's Ropeworks. The public house was owned by Whitmore, a Royston brewery, in the early years of the century. It was managed by Mrs. Lewin and her husband was a jobbing gardener. The Prince had a good reputation and was well-known for the fine accommodation that it offered to both people and horses! This corner was looked upon as the hub of the village and it was here that the village notice board stood next to the Jubilee Pump.

57. The year is 1919, the Great War is over, and village life continues with its seasonal activities. Here is a group of around fifty people waiting for a char-à-banc to take them on the Chapel outing to Royston Heath, a spot some twelve miles distant which offered a contrast to the flat meadowland of home. The village pump stands within a small fenced enclosure to the left of the group. According to Fanny Wale it 'was placed there to commemorate the first jubilee of Queen Victoria. The well is bored down 50 feet to reach the pure water below the stratum of white chalk'. In the days when very few houses had their own piped water supply the daily chore of fetching buckets of water from the village pump was one that was shared between all members of the family.

58. Here at the junction of Church Street and Hauxton Road two men stand beside their pony and trap. Behind them is the pantiled roof of the Smithy and the gates that opened onto the blacksmith's yard, where much of his work was carried out – like most country folk preferring to work outside – weather permitting. The blacksmith at this time was Edward Elbourne, who had learnt his craft from a boy working at his father's side. The blacksmith was an invaluable member of the village community. He could shoe the horses, repair the machinery, repair and sometimes make cartwheels, fashion smaller items such as latches and light fittings for the home, repair garden tools, make gates, in fact, for anything involving the use of iron – the village blacksmith was your man!

59. In this old photograph we see Edward Elbourne and his two sons, Charlie and Malcolm, lowering the iron tyre onto the wooden part of the cartwheel. These wooden sections, the hub, the spokes and the wooden rim, probably made by the local carpenter, were set up on a circular iron platform. The iron tyre, which had already been made to the correct size, was heated until red hot over an open fire, which can be seen in the background. It took three men using a long-handled, hooked tool to lift the tyre from the fire onto the wheel. Then there were a frantic few minutes when water had to be poured on the rim to prevent the woodwork from catching fire and to cause the iron tyre to cool and shrink more quickly (note the cans of water standing ready). A cartwheel could be re-tyred several times during its lifetime.

Mount View Cottages Lt Shelford

60. There was a right of way through the blacksmith's yard to the Garden Fields. This area of land was once the village recreation ground, but in 1880 Col. K.G. Wale decided that it would be more beneficial for the ground to be used as allotment gardens, because many of the people living in the smaller cottages had large families but very little space on which to grow vegetables. So the name of Garden Fields arose. Mount View Cottages were built on some of this ground (possibly in the late 1920's) by a local builder, Frederick Albert Marshall, who lived on the corner of Newton Road. Their name of course was derived from the view of Maggots Mount from this area.

High St., Little Shelford

61. And so we turn into High Street and just a short distance past the hawthorn hedge that borders the western end of Camping Close we come to the house of Charles Butler, baker and confectioner. A business that has been carried on through the generations, with all members of the family being involved in either baking, delivering of serving in the shop. In addition to the shop, attached to the family home, Mr. Butler also had a shop in Woollard's Lane, Great Shelford, for some time. The bakehouse was at the rear of this house. Next door lived the blacksmith, Mr. Elbourne, and his family. He was very much involved in the life of the village, as he was also churchwarden and a village constable.

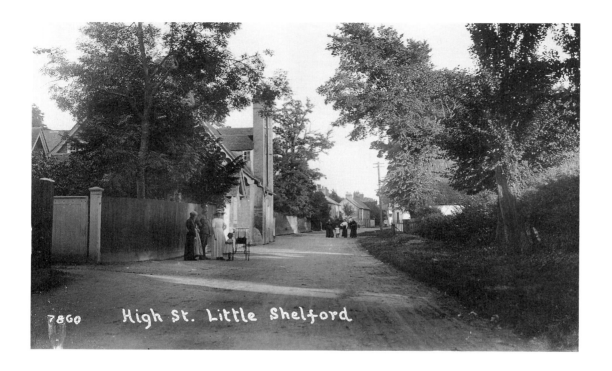

7860 High St. Little Shelford

62. The next building down the street is King's Farm, a house which originated as a small cottage, but was altered in the late 18th century and then greatly enlarged at the beginning of this century to designs by Frederick Lean. The house stands end onto the road with the kitchen chimney projecting onto the high-way. This chimney provided a warm corner for courting couples on a cold winter's night! The photograph was taken c1915 and a soldier (possibly Mr. Goodwin) is home on leave and out walking with his family down a peaceful village street − a stark contrast to life at the Front. On the right is the meadow of White's Farm, but we cannot see through the dense hedge to know what is grazing there.

7854 King's Farm Little Shelford.

63. Here we can see the front of King's Farm, roses rambling around the windows and a splendid car awaiting its driver. During the first thirty years of this century there were four different occupants of King's Farm. Mr. John Eaden, then Lt. Col. Thornton, followed by Gerald Fitzgerald and then by 1930 Henry Bayon were in residence. King's Farm was part of the Wale estate and on his death in 1796 at the age of 95 Thomas Wale left this farm to his daughter Margaretta, and after the inclosure of 1815 she owned about 140 acres. The line of inheritance includes names which are familiar in the village even now — Eaden, Willis, Powell — but much of the land has now been sold, either to be developed or to be attached to the acreages of neighbouring farms.

7859   High St. Little Shelford

64. Three generations of the Litchfield family stand outside White's Farmhouse, c1922. In the foreground stands Francis and Elizabeth Litchfield's eldest married daughter, Annie, with her daughter Doris. Annie was married to Elias Townsend, who was landlord of the Prince Regent at this time. Two of the farm workers have also got into the picture as they stand behind the wooden fence that surrounds the small garden of Hubert Flitton, the horsekeeper. On the extreme left can be seen the wall of Kirby Lodge. Mr. Abbott lived there in 1900 and later on Mrs. Thompson and then Mrs. Hudson were in residence. On the right, partially blocked by the garden wall, can be seen the back of King's Farm.

65. Harvest time – the culmination of the farmer's year – was a busy time for both men and horses. Here Frank and Reuben Litchfield work with their team of horses to cut the barley with a binder in the field behind White's Farm. The binder was intended to be pulled by a pair of horses, but with a third one harnessed-up alongside, the intention was probably to lighten the load so that the animals could work a longer day. Sometimes this idea was used to train a young animal to work and gain experience with older horses. The care of harness was a major preoccupation on the farm for without reliable harness a good horse was rendered useless. Leather straps and collars were wiped with Neatsfoot oil and chains and other metal parts were washed. A harness-maker from Balsham visited White's Farm for a week each year to overhaul the harness.

Little Shelford Works

66. Mr. and Mrs. William Rogers lived in one of these houses in the terrace along the High Street. In 1906 Mrs. Rogers posted this card to her daughter in Bedford Square in London to say '… am sending off parcel, hope you will get it tonight'. What a good delivery service for both postcard and parcel. This row of houses was built around 1870 when there was a demand for more labourers' cottages to accommodate the growing population. The 1891 census returns show that Mr. Rogers, who gave his occupation as gardener and gamekeeper, had the largest family to occupy these two up and two down cottages. In 1891 he had eight children living at home aged between 17 and 1 year. It must have been a tight squeeze around the table at mealtimes, and again when bedtime came around.

67. Edward Moore was landlord of the Plough Inn for over thirty years. His stepfather Charles Jennings lived next door and in the yard behind the house stood a small bakery. Ted Moore baked bread here in the early years of the century and sold it from a cart around the village. The public house is easily recognisable today and it is one of the two remaining inns in the village. Sadly, however, the name has been changed to The Navigator, apparently to avoid confusion with the Plough at Great Shelford.

68. This photograph taken outside the Carrier's Cart (or Carrier's Arms) c1890 shows the landlady, Mrs. Maryann Watkins, and members of her family. Maryann had previously been Mrs. Litchfield and upon the premature death of her husband, James, which left her with three young children − the youngest only six months old − she decided that she would continue to run the beerhouse and also her late husband's carrier's business. She was widowed for a second time and her third marriage was to Fred Dockrell, who had returned from the gold fields in Australia to his native village with enough money to buy the Carrier's Cart from Phillip's Brewery of Royston. Francis Litchfield is in the cart, Reuben Goat holds the horse's head and the ladies from the left are: Maryann, Elizabeth Goat, Elizabeth Litchfield and Clara Jennings (neighbour).

The Terrace Lt Shelford.

69. The Terrace is a footpath that links High Street with the Whittlesford Road. It got its name from the terrace of thatched cottages that bordered this footpath at the High Street end. These can be seen in this photograph, but sadly, together with the pantiled houses in the distance, they have been demolished. Across the road stands Hall Farm, an early 16th century building which was extended in the 17th and 18th centuries. John Fordham came from Fen Ditton to take over the tenancy in 1889 and succeeding generations still farm the land today. Their cattle, which graze in the meadows at the southern end of the village, are a poignant reminder of the days when every farm had its selection of animals.

A Quaint Spot, Lt Shelford.

135b83

70. Now on the road to Hauxton we look back towards the Prince Regent corner. A variety of cottages can be seen on both sides of the road. The majority have pantiled roofs with the exception of the cottage in the centre of the picture which is situated on the corner of Church Street and High Street and this has a straw thatch. We look back in more ways than one, because this truly is a view of Little Shelford past, for the last of these houses was demolished some twenty years ago.

8259 - Hauxton Rd. Lt Shelford.

71. This thatched cottage on the corner of Newton Road was the home of Frederick Marshall, who was responsible for the building of Mount View Cottages. His ladders, stored on brackets under the deep thatch of his house, give some indication of his trade. Another local builder at the beginning of the century was Arthur Austin, whose family had been long established in the area as windmill builders. Towards the end of the last century he built a brewery in Hauxton Road, which can be seen in this picture beyond the trees. It was known as the West End Brewery, but it was not a great success — perhaps it could not compete with the larger brewers — and by 1916 the premises were no longer used for this purpose. The buildings were demolished by 1966.

72. The two milkmen from Manor Farm Dairy pause for Mr. Mott in Hauxton Road. They have been identified as Mr. Amey, on the left, and, holding the horse's head, Henry Ellis. They each carry a gallon can which would have been refilled from the large churn carried in the milk float. When taken to each door the quantity of milk required would be ladled into a jug provided by the householder. Sometimes milk was delivered twice a day to coincide with the morning and afternoon milking of the cows. This ensured fresh milk to the housewife even in the hottest of summers and in these days before refrigeration there were few complaints about milk turning sour. At this time, c1920, a pint of milk cost 2d, or ½d less if collected from the farm.

Hauxton Level Crossing, Little Shelford.

73. Further along Hauxton Road, towards the northern boundary of the parish, is the level crossing over the Cambridge to King's Cross railway line. This line was opened in 1851 but at this time it terminated at Royston and was extended at a later date to go right into London. The district nurse in her uniform is crossing the line, the large wicker basket on her bicycle handlebars a necessity in her profession. Could this be Miss Laura May, who was for some time the district nurse in the area? The butcher's boy on his trade bike is returning to Great Shelford after making a delivery to Hauxton. The Crossing House stood on the left of the gates and it was here that the employee of the Great Northern Railway lived who would either man the gates or work in the signalbox.

7552. Newton Rd. Little Shelford.

74. Another road leading out of the village is the Newton Road: just a narrow country lane at the time of the photograph with wide grass verges and overgrown hedges, with a few large houses at the village end of the road. Further out, towards Newton and Harston, stood Moor Barns Farm with its isolated cottages and further on still, merging with Harston, was the gamekeeper's house. This northern end of the village is now crossed by the M11 motorway, which sweeps across the horizon and dwarfs Newton and Hauxton Roads with its towering bridges and embankments.

7870　Red House. Little Shelford

75. One of the larger houses built towards the end of the last century was the Red House which is situated in Newton Road. Mr. George Bagnall lived there for well over twenty years and he was well known as a successful cultivator of mushrooms and asparagus. Another large house which was erected during the last century was Saintfoins in Whittlesford Road. This was bought by Hamer Towgood in 1860 and he lived there until his death in 1914. Mr. Alfred Peart bought Saintfoins in June 1914 for £2,000. A few months later, whilst alterations were being made, there was a serious fire, the house was burnt out and only the walls were left standing. However, Mr. Peart persevered and the house was rebuilt for his occupation.

8267 Meregots Mount, Little Shelford

76. 'He lived an advocate for liberty, a good subject, an agreeable companion, a faithful friend, an hospitable neighbour and in all parts of life a useful member of society.' This is part of the engraving to be found on the obelisk which is situated on St. Margaret's Mount, or Maggots Mount, a high vantage point to the west of the village that can be reached by a footpath from Newton Road. It was erected in 1739 to the memory of Mr. Gregory Wale by his friend, James Church. They regularly met at this place on horseback over many years and agreed that whoever should live the longest, would erect a memorial to their friendship on this high ground overlooking the parish. It was Mr. Church who lived to carry out this pact.